St. Patrick's Day
SHAMROCKS

St. Patrick's Day
SHAMROCKS

Mary Berendes

THE CHILD'S WORLD®, INC.

Library of Congress Cataloging-in-Publication Data
Berendes, Mary.
St. Patrick's Day shamrocks / by Mary Berendes.
p.   cm.
Includes index.
Summary: Describes the tiny green plants
known as shamrocks, the customs and origins
of St. Patrick's Day, and how the shamrock
became the national symbol of Ireland.
ISBN 1-56766-643-4 (Library reinforced : alk paper)
1. Saint Patrick's Day—Juvenile literature.   2. Clover—Juvenile literature.
3. Shamrock (Emblem)—Juvenile literature.
[1. Saint Patrick's Day. 2. Clover. 3. Shamrock (Emblem).]
I. Title. II. Title: St. Patrick's Day shamrocks.
GT4995.P3B47   1997
394.262—dc21   98-56521
CIP
AC

Photo Credits

© Andrew N. Gagg's PHOTO FLORA: 15
© ARCHIVE PHOTOS: 23, 24
© CORBIS/Bill Ross: 30
© CORBIS/Charles W. Campbell: 2
© David N. Davis: cover
© 1997 DPA/Dembinsky Photo Assoc. Inc.: 19
© John Kehely/KeeWi Photography: 9, 26, 29
© Ken Biggs/Tony Stone Images: 20
© 1997 Kent Wood: 13
© Lambert/ARCHIVE PHOTOS: 6
© 1997 Ron Sherman: 16
© Walt Anderson: 10

On the cover...

Front cover: These bright green clover plants are growing in a quiet area.
Page 2: Some people think plants like this *redwood sorrel* are shamrocks.

Table of Contents

Everywhere you look on St. Patrick's Day, there are green decorations. If you look closely, you will see that many decorations are shaped like tiny green plants. Each leaf of these plants has three parts with round edges. What are these strange-looking plants? They're shamrocks!

What Are Shamrocks?

Shamrocks are **trefoils,** or plants that have leaves with three parts. Clover plants and some lotus plants are also trefoils. Other than being trefoils, no one is really sure what shamrocks are! Some people say shamrocks are a plant called a *hop clover.* Others think shamrocks are really *black medic* plants that grow in certain areas of Europe and Asia. Still others think that *sorrel* plants are the true shamrocks.

These *yellow clover* plants are growing in a forest in Ireland. ⇒

Most people, though, think that the *white clover* is the real shamrock plant. It has skinny green stems and pink or white flowers. It has round green leaves, too.

White clover grows best in wet areas. That's because its **roots** are very short. A plant's roots grow in the soil and soak up water. Since clover roots don't grow very deep, clover can only grow in areas where the water stays near the surface.

Why Are Shamrocks Green?

Like most plants, shamrocks are green. They get their color from something called **chlorophyll** (KLOR–uh–fill). Chlorophyll is a green coloring found in almost every part of a plant. It is important because it lets plants soak up energy from the sun.

The dark spots inside these plant cells show areas with chlorophyll. ⇒

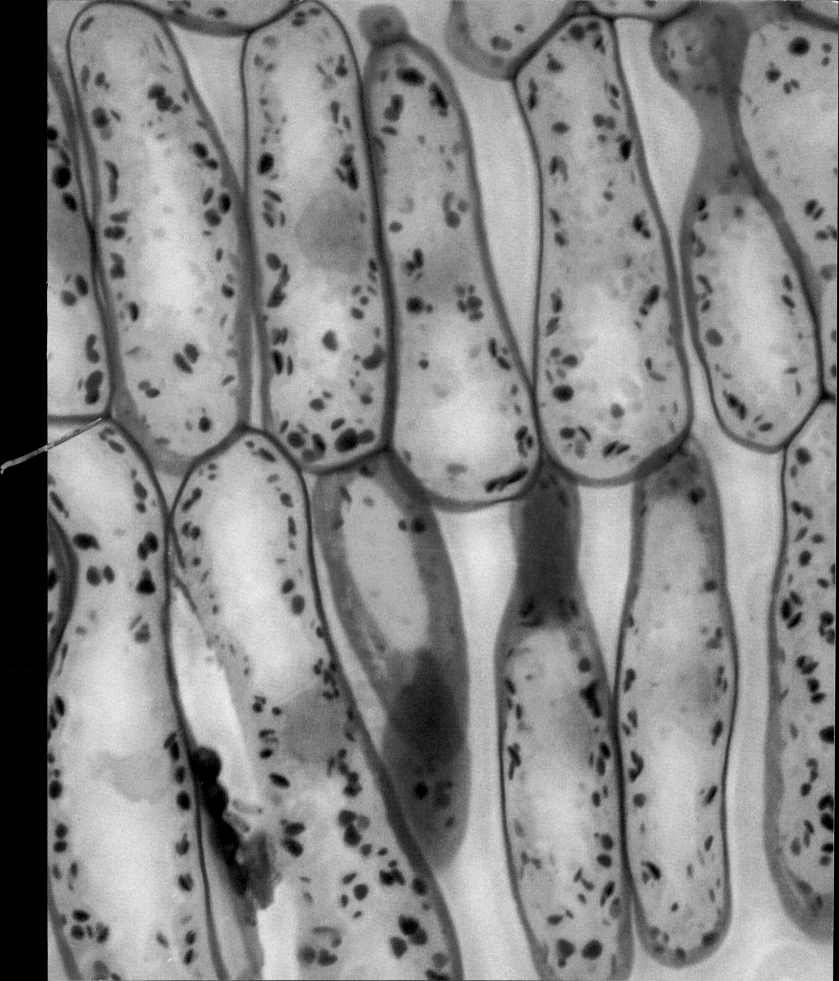

If plants couldn't soak up sunshine, they would die. That is because they need sunshine to make food! The process green plants use to make food is called **photosynthesis** (foh–toh–SIN–thuh–sis). In photosynthesis, energy from the sun is mixed with air and water to make food for the plant. Without the green chlorophyll to soak up the sunshine, most of the plants on Earth would starve.

These white clover plants are gathering energy from the sunshine. ⇒

St. Patrick's Day happens every year on March 17. On that day, people celebrate Ireland, Irish people, and a man who was good and kind to others. This man, called **Saint Patrick,** lived in Ireland more than 1,500 years ago.

On St. Patrick's Day, people wear green clothes to remember the green grasses and fields of Ireland. Some cities hold parades and have parties with lots of Irish music. Some people cook foods that come from Ireland, too. Most of all, green shamrocks can be seen everywhere.

⇐ This mother and son are watching a St. Patrick's Day parade.

Who Was St. Patrick?

More than 1,500 years ago, a boy named Patrick was born in what is now western Britain. As a child, Patrick was happy. But when he was 16 years old, Patrick was kidnapped by pirates who were attacking his city. He was taken on a ship and sold to work as a slave in Ireland.

St. Patrick worked as a shepherd in Irish fields and hills like these. ⇒

Patrick was a slave for six years. He was very unhappy and missed his family in Britain. To keep his spirits up, Patrick started to think about God. He prayed that one day God would help him get free.

Then one night, Patrick had a dream. In his dream, God told Patrick that there was a ship that would take him home. He quickly awoke and escaped that very night. After walking for a few days, Patrick found a ship that was sailing to Britain.

After many weeks, Patrick at last came home. His parents were overjoyed and told him never to leave again. But soon Patrick had another dream. In this dream, he felt God told him that the people of Ireland needed his help. They needed someone to teach them and pray with them. Patrick knew what he had to do. He went to a **monastery,** a place where he could study and learn more about God. Then he sailed back to Ireland.

This very old drawing shows St. Patrick after his return to Ireland. ⇒

Back in Ireland, Patrick began to teach people about God. He talked and preached and told stories about God to anyone who would listen. He helped build churches and schools, too. Soon people everywhere began to hear about him. They began telling stories about Patrick to their friends and neighbors. These stories, called **legends,** are still known today.

The best-known legend about St. Patrick involves the shamrock. While learning at the monastery, Patrick was taught an idea about God. His teachers told him that God was made of three beings. When he preached in Ireland, the people did not understand this idea. To help, Patrick reached down to the ground and plucked a shamrock. He told the people that God's three parts were like the three parts of the shamrock's leaf. Legend has it that from then on, the shamrock became the national symbol of Ireland.

⇐ This yellow clover plant is growing in the sunshine.

Are Shamrocks Lucky?

Long ago, people thought shamrocks had magical powers. They thought this because the shamrock's leaves stand up when a storm is coming. Over time, people learned that this really wasn't magic at all. It was just the way shamrocks respond to changing weather.

Today, some people see shamrocks as lucky plants. People feel that shamrocks, just like lucky pennies found on the street, can keep them happy and healthy.

This white clover plant is growing in a quiet forest in Ireland. ⇒

Today, the shamrock is a symbol of Ireland. The green color of the shamrock reminds people of the beautiful green fields of Ireland. It also reminds people with Irish relatives of the place from which their family members came. Even if you don't believe in the legend of the first shamrock, they are still fun to decorate with on St. Patrick's Day!

Glossary

chlorophyll (KLOR–uh–fill)
Chlorophyll is a green coloring found in most plants. It lets the plants soak up energy from the sun to make food.

legends (LEH–jendz)
Legends are stories that are passed on from person to person. There are several legends about St. Patrick.

monastery (MAH–nuh–stayr–ee)
A monastery is a place where people go to live and learn about God. St. Patrick learned about God in a monastery before he returned to Ireland.

photosynthesis (foh–toh–SIN–thuh–sis)
Photosynthesis is the process that green plants use to make food. Shamrocks use photosynthesis.

roots (ROOTS)
Roots are the parts of a plant that grow underground. Clover plants have short roots.

Saint Patrick (SAYNT PA–trik)
Saint Patrick was a man who preached about God in Ireland more than 1,500 years ago. Saint Patrick used a shamrock to explain an idea about God to the Irish people.

trefoils (TREE–foylz)
A trefoil is a plant that has leaves with three parts. Shamrocks are trefoils.

Index